Vera

Sally

Plate 1

Irene   Mary

Plate 2

V

S

do not cut
out white
areas
between
arms
and
body

Plate 3

I

M

do not cut out
white area
between
arm and body

Plate 4

Plate 5

Plate 6

Buddy

Wallace

Plate 7

V

S

Plate 8

do not
cut out
white area
between arm
and body

I

I

M

Plate 9

Charles

Buster

Plate 10

V

S

Plate 11

I

I

M

M

Plate 12

V

V

do not cut out
white area
between arm
and body

I

Plate 13

Plate 14

V

S

S

Plate 15